RUNOUTS

MARY TIPTON

CONSULTANT · LINDSAY JOHN BRADSHAW

BASED ON · COURSE · CITY AND GUILDS SUGARCRAFT

MEREHURST

The author is indebted to her colleagues Peggy McMahon, Sue Poole and John Waterhouse for all their unstinting help. Advice, ideas and support from Beryl Lane, Sarah Matthews, Florence Pearce, Margaret Rowe and Martin Thomson are also gratefully acknowledged.

≈

Published in 1991 by Merehurst Limited, Ferry House, 51–57 Lacy Road, Putney, London SW15 1PR.

Reprinted 1993

Copyright © Merehurst Limited 1991

ISBN 1 85391 216 6

Edited by Jenni Fleetwood
Designed by Peter Bridgewater
Photographs by Ken Field
Colour Separation by Fotographics Ltd.
UK – Hong Kong
Printed in Hong Kong by Wing King Tong Ltd.

The author and publishers would like to thank the following for their assistance:
Cornish Cakeboards, Rosehill, Goonhavern, Truro, Cornwall TR4 9JT; House of Cakes, 18 Meadow Close, Woodley, Stockport, Cheshire, SK6 1QZ; Jane Adele Flowers, P.S. Compton Castle, Back Quay, Truro, Cornwall, TR1 2LW.
Lettering on page 69 © 1972 Esselte Letraset Ltd.

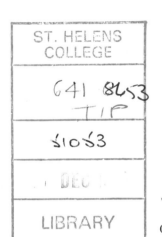
NOTES ON USING THE RECIPES
For all recipes, quantities are given in metric, Imperial and cup measurements. Follow one set of measures only as they are not interchangeable. Standard 5ml teaspoons (tsp) and 15ml tablespoons (tbsp) are used. Australian readers, whose tablespoons measure 20ml, should adjust quantities accordingly. All spoon measures are assumed to be level unless otherwise stated.
Ovens should be pre-heated to specified temperature.
Eggs are a standard size 3 unless otherwise stated.
Quantities of icing used on cakes are approximate.

CONTENTS

INTRODUCTION

Having mastered basic coating and piping, the budding artist in sugar is usually tempted to try runout work. This type of sugar decoration has maintained its popularity for around 70 years, the style changing with the times. Basically, runout, or soft sugar, work is prefabricated decoration carried out with softened royal icing which has been dried on wax paper, the paper being removed before the item is attached to the cake.

Runout skills are a versatile addition to the cake decorator's resources. For borders, runouts can be used to give a clean, crisp appearance particularly suitable for formal cakes; at the same time making the cake appear larger. They are ideal for plaques and inscriptions which can be made in advance and stored for use at short notice, and they are also popular for creating figures and ornamental pieces ranging from butterflies to buildings.

The classic English example of the method, with runout top and bottom collars, runout ornaments, and often, side panels, has its own elegant beauty - when it is done well. It is however, a daunting project for the beginner to runout work.

This book has been designed to take the reader through a series of exercises introducing progressively more difficult techniques so that by the time he or she has reached the last page a comprehensive range of intermediate runout skills has been covered.

The amount of runout work included ranges from simple plaques to curved pieces and more intricate designs. Detailed step-by-step instructions and templates are provided so that the cakes illustrated can be reproduced or the designs adapted to suit the reader's own level of skill.

It is hoped that the cake decorator who has worked his or her way through this book will have enjoyed acquiring new skills and will be inspired to graduate to tackling the advanced areas of filigree panels and floating collars.

*M*uch of the equipment required for runout work will probably already be in your toolbox, but since this is one type of sugar work which will not wait while you search for a particular implement, it is a good idea to keep a list of essential items on a small card with your tools so that you can collect them all together easily before starting work.

DRYING BOARDS Any flat surface unaffected by heat is suitable. Wooden boards, cake boards, glazed tiles, perspex (plexiglass) and glass all may be used.

DESIGNS These can be drawn, traced or photocopied on firm paper, but the lines should be simple and clear. Suggestions - and templates - are given throughout this book. Thin papers, such as greaseproof (parchment) or tracing paper, are not suitable since they have a tendency to curl when subjected to the heat necessary for drying the pieces. Cartridge paper is ideal. Avoid using wax paper *directly* on glazed tiles or glass. If the runout is exposed to direct heat for too long, or if the heat source is too close, the warmth may melt the wax in the paper and bond it to the tile when cool.

MASKING TAPE This is needed for taping designs to the drying board. This type of tape is the easiest to remove once the runout pieces have dried. Drawing pins may be used with some boards.

PAPER/FILM There are many grades of wax paper available. It should be flat and crease-free. If you buy wax paper by the roll, cut it into large squares (25-30cm/10-12 in), place between two 30cm (12 in) cake boards and put a weight on top to flatten the pieces. Specially treated reusable materials for runout work are now available. These are worth investigating although they lack fineness and can be difficult to see through. Cooking film is another material which is popular. It has the twin advantages of being fine while not melting under heat, but light can create an uncomfortable glare from the surface. The choice of paper/film is a personal one and may simply depend on what is available. Be careful not to select a permeable paper which will make your runouts run!

GREASEPROOF OR NON-STICK PAPER PIPING BAGS These can be purchased ready-made or made at home. Small bags will be useful for outlines, while small or medium bags will be required for run-icing. Other essential pieces of equipment include scissors, No. 1 and 2 piping tubes (tips), small water pot, small mixing bowl with airtight lid or damp cloth for covering and a wide-necked bottle or jar to hold bags while filling with run-icing.

ANGLED LAMP To dry the runout rapidly, an angled desk lamp is required: a 60-watt bulb will give sufficient heat if it can be angled to a few inches above the runout. A spotlight or reflector bulb (also 60 watt) will provide a little more heat. When the runouts are dry, you will find it helpful to invert them on a sheet of foam for protection while the paper is being removed.

Other than items specified in individual recipes throughout this book, the basic equipment illustrated right is essential for successful runout work.

Clockwise, from top left:- sheet of foam, desk lamp, albumen solution, wax paper, wide-necked bottle, re-usable film, assorted drying boards, small palette knife, masking tape, piping tubes (tips), paste colours, paper piping bags, scissors, paintbrushes, powder colours, water pot.

Like many other sugarcraft skills, runouts can be simple or elaborate, from a basic white plaque to a brightly coloured figure with rounded limbs, or an exquisite collar. All use the same basic technique, namely flooding a given area with royal icing. The consistency of the icing may vary slightly; the figures may or may not be outlined, but the principle is the same. Step-by-step instructions for basic runout work are given on pages 10-11. For outlines, freshly beaten royal icing is used full strength in a small bag fitted with a no. 1 tube (tip). The icing should not be more than 2-3 days old, and should be paddled on a spotlessly clean board to just below full peak consistency immediately before use. The technique is the same as that used when spreading icing on a cake; a stiff palette knife is used to push the icing first in one direction and then in the other, to break down any air bubbles. The icing used for flooding - run-icing - requires stronger albumen than regular royal icing. The best way of achieving this is by using powdered albumen instead of liquid egg white; the proportion of powdered albumen can be increased without making the icing too fluid, see recipe.

It is not always convenient to make up a special icing for runout work, however. If you are flat icing a cake in royal icing, you will obviously prefer to use the same icing for any runouts. You *can* use your usual royal icing recipe, but should thin it with more albumen, using either albumen solution or egg white, depending on your original recipe. To make albumen solution for runouts, reconstitute 4 tsp powdered albumen in 7 tsp water. Stir in 1 tsp of the liquid at a time, taking care to avoid beating in air bubbles. Icing of the correct consistency will hold a trail that disappears when the bowl is gently tapped on the work surface.

For coloured runouts, colour the royal icing before thinning it. Mix the colour through well to prevent streaking or colour migration. Liquid, paste and powder food colourings are suitable but be careful when using paste colours that contain glycerol (glycerine), particularly if you are trying to create deep shades, see Glossary page 71. Glycerol is hygroscopic; used in large quantities it will prevent the runout from drying satisfactorily. Mix deep tones a shade lighter than required as colour will develop as icing dries.

The basic technique is as follows: Prepare several greaseproof paper (parchment) piping bags, fitting them with no. 2 tubes (tips), if liked. Fill each bag with run-icing as indicated in step 2 on page 11. If no tube has been fitted, cut the tip of each bag after filling. The icing should flow smoothly but the hole should be small enough to burst most of the air bubbles that are forced through it. Avoid working with the same bag for too long, as the warmth of your hand will alter the structure of the icing. Work in a cool but not damp atmosphere to allow time for flooding each piece carefully, but as soon as the runout is ready, place it under a lamp to dry surface crystals quickly and create the characteristic sheen. Store completed runouts flat in a warm, dry atmosphere.

ROYAL ICING FOR RUNOUTS

❖

Use this icing for outlines. To make run-icing, thin it with water.

60g (2 oz/¼ cup) powdered albumen
reconstituted in
280ml (10 fl oz/1¼ cups) water
1.75kg (3½ lb/10½ cups) icing
(confectioners') sugar

Make up the albumen solution in a grease-free bowl. Add three quarters of the icing (confectioners') sugar and beat with an electric mixer for 2 minutes on slow speed. Adjust consistency with remaining sugar and beat for 3 minutes more on slow speed until icing peaks. Makes about 1.75kg (3½ lb).
NOTE For a small quantity, mix 4 tsp powdered albumen with 7 tsp water and add 220g (7 oz) icing (confectioners') sugar.

PLAQUES

*T*he simplest type of runout work for the newcomer to the skill to attempt is the plaque. These are prefabricated runout shapes which can be made in advance and used on cakes to display bought, modelled or runout ornaments. They may be embellished, see page 12, used in conjunction with inscriptions or monograms, or painted with food colours.

Plaques provide the ideal introduction to basic runout technique; it is worth spending a little time mastering the skill before moving on to more complicated designs. Familiarise yourself with the basic technique, described on page 8, assemble the necessary equipment, see page 6, and follow the simple step-by-step instructions opposite.

Once drawings are prepared and the basic technique has been mastered, plaques can be mass produced quite quickly, see pages 22-23. It is useful to have a small stock to turn to for short notice orders. The shape of the plaque is limited only by your imagination.

Templates for some of the more popular styles of plaque are on pages 56-57.

QUICK TIPS

- Use a spray of bought silk flowers to decorate a plaque, adding individuality by rearranging the flowers, curving leaves and incorporating your own ribbon bows or loops.
- Arrange a single sugar, wafer or silk flower or a small ornament. Add a piped inscription.
- Model an animal in marzipan (almond paste) or sugarpaste and mount on a plaque for a child's birthday cake.
- Keep a supply of silvered plastic initials for personalising cakes. If time permits, use piped or runout letters instead. For emphasis, use plaques for initial letters of inscriptions, see pages 14-15.

~ 1 ~

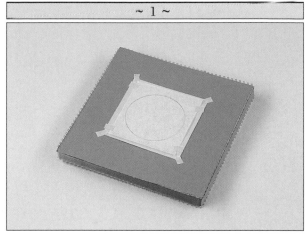

Templates for plaques are on pages 56-57. Trace chosen design (or design of own choice) and fix to drying board with masking tape or drawing pins. Cut a piece of wax paper slightly larger than drawing; fix it in place with masking tape or drawing pins. Make sure wax surface is uppermost and that pieces of paper are flat.

~ 4 ~

Pipe a line of run-icing as close as possible to outline. If there are any gaps, tease icing out with a paintbrush. Continue to flood remaining area, maintaining a steady pressure on the bag so that the icing is gently forced through the tip, rather than allowed to flow out. Keep end of bag in icing.

~ 2 ~

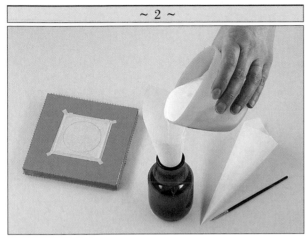

Select a medium bag with or without a no. 2 tube (tip), see page 8, and support it in a wide-necked bottle or jar. Prepare a batch of run-icing, see page 8. Pour run-icing into bag until half full. Fold down top tightly. If no tube was used, cut end of bag to the size of a no. 2 tube.

~ 3 ~

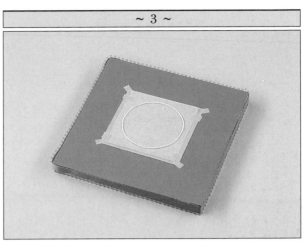

Have ready a small paper piping bag fitted with a no. 1 tube (tip) and filled with royal icing. Using a no. 1 tube and royal icing in a small bag, outline design. Make sure any joins are neat; touching each other but not overlapping.

~ 5 ~

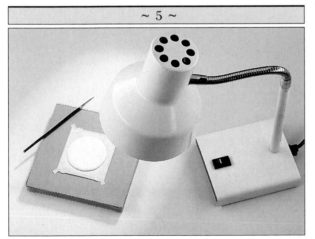

Gently tap drying board on surface to level run-icing. Any air bubbles rising to the surface can be burst with the tip of a paintbrush. Place plaque or other runout design under an angled desk lamp to dry.

~ 6 ~

When you are ready to use the runout, place it face down on a piece of foam and carefully peel off wax paper. Pipe a line or some dots of royal icing on reverse and position piece right-way-up on cake.

LETTERING, NUMERALS & EMBELLISHMENTS

LETTERING & NUMERALS

❖

Runouts lend an importance to lettering, monograms and numerals. Here again, contrasts in colour can be used to create interesting effects. Coloured outlines are not difficult to do and they seem to bring letters to life. Letters or numerals can be flooded with two or more different colours, if liked. Flood them at the same time to get a merged effect or allow one colour to dry before flooding the next for a crisper look. Multicoloured lettering looks especially effective on children's cakes.

Another technique is to flood the letters in one colour and add shading when the letters are dry. This can be done using dusting powder (petal dust/blossom tint) on a soft brush, or by spraying. For spraying, use a stiff brush such as a new toothbrush, dipped in liquid colour. Hold the brush above the letters with the bristles pointing downward, then run a clean finger firmly across the bristles. Alternatively, use an airbrush (see Glossary, page 71).

Lettering for monograms needs to be wider-bodied than lettering for piping. One such alphabet is shown on page 66 and you will also find many suitable examples in other cake decorating or lettering books. Letters with thick and thin parts to their bodies seem to adapt best for monograms; you need to experiment to find the best way of entwining two letters.

Trace both letters on separate pieces of paper, then place one tracing on top of the other and slide the letters about until a pleasing arrangement is found. Make a tracing of that arrangement and use that as the basis for your working drawing. In general, a monogram looks better when the thin parts of one letter appear to lie behind a thicker part of its associated letter.

To fix a runout letter or numeral to a cake or plaque, pipe a few dots of icing on the reverse and position it carefully.

EMBELLISHMENTS

❖

When dry, plaques may be embellished with tiny dots of icing - sometimes known as *microdots*. There are several patterns for these, the most usual being illustrated opposite. The technique is also used on runout border pieces and collars.

Microdots are piped using a no. 1 or no. 0 tube (tip) and royal icing of soft peak consistency, which when piped forms a soft rounded shape with no visible peaks. Ease the wax paper away from the edges of the dry plaque, but don't remove it completely. Angle the tube so that the dots are piped partly on the outline of the runout and partly on the wax paper. When completed, dot sequences should lie level with the edge of the runout and not be raised at an angle from it. If you rest the end of the tube on the paper as you pipe all the dots should be level.

Other methods can be used to give attractive edgings to plaques and collars. Outlining in a contrasting colour can look effective: Use a no. 1 tube (tip) for outlining, allowing the icing to crust over before flooding with run-icing. When flooding, take care not to cover the outline. Metallic effects can be painted over the outline before flooding commences.

Another edging, piped picot, is used on the bottom border of the Valentine's Day Cake illustrated on page 53. On a plaque or collar, this may be piped in a self-colour or a contrast. Use a no. 1 tube (tip) and make sure you make contact with the edge of the runout while piping. Tiny scroll edging and simple piped lace may also be used as decorative finishes on plaques.

~ 1 ~

LETTERS/NUMERALS *Pipe coloured outlines with royal icing; allow to dry before flooding in with run-icing in a paler colour. Paint gold and silver edges over a plain outline that has been allowed to dry. When gold and silver edges are dry, flood the body of the runout.*

~ 2 ~

Interesting effects can be created by flooding in different colours or by decorating letters and numerals when dry.

~ 3 ~

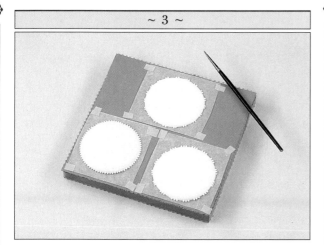

EMBELLISHMENTS *The one-dot edging/ embellishment is illustrated left. Top plaque shows the first stage of the 3-dot sequence. Dots are piped in pairs around the plaque. These should not be touching, but there should not be enough room between them to pipe another dot. The same technique is used for start of 6-dot sequence (right), but dots are piped in threes.*

~ 4 ~

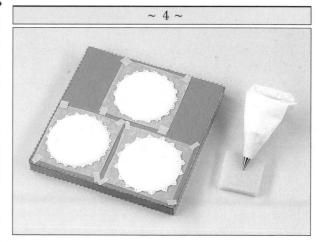

Plaque on left shows completion of 3-dot sequence, with a third dot straddling the paired dots to create a pyramid effect. The second and third stages of the 6-dot sequence are shown top and right. Pyramid effect is created first by piping two dots between and ahead of trio, then crowning each pyramid with a final dot. Allow each stage to dry before going on to the next.

TWIN HEART
ENGAGEMENT CAKE

The simple plaques and capital letters on this cake provide a gentle introduction to runout skills for even the most timid decorator. The design is one which can readily be adapted for an anniversary or a small wedding - just change the colour scheme and ornaments as appropriate. Trimming the cakes and covering them separately makes them easier to handle, both while they are being decorated and when they are being cut up.

two 20cm (8 in) heart-shaped cakes
apricot glaze
1.75kg (3½ lb) marzipan (almond paste)
clear alcohol (gin or vodka)
2kg (4 lb) pale peach sugarpaste
selection of food colourings
royal icing
albumen solution for run-icing
E Q U I P M E N T
38cm (15 in) square cake board
embossing tool, optional
scriber
large plain crimper
runout equipment, see page 6
no, 1, 3, 42 and 2 piping tubes (tips)
sugar or silk floral spray
keepsake ornament, optional
about 1.5cm (1¾ yd) ribbon or paper band for board edge

● Cut matching sections, 11cm (4½ in) long, from right side of one cake and left side of the other, so that when assembled side by side they fit together neatly. Brush both cakes with apricot glaze and cover with marzipan (almond paste). Brush with alcohol. Cover cakes and board with sugarpaste. Emboss board edges, if liked.
● Make a greaseproof paper (parchment) template for side of each cake, fold each template into eight equal sections and cut a scalloped design for bottom border. Fix a template to the side of each cake and scribe scallop design. Use crimper to mark a scalloped design at top edge of each cake: open out crimper and press one end into paste to lightly emboss shape.
● When dry, position cakes on board. Make three small runout plaques, following instructions on page 10 and using template on page 56. Make runout capital letters for each initial and for E of Engagement, following technique under Letters/Numerals on page 13 and using alphabet on page 66. When plaques are dry, pipe cornelli work over them, using a no. 1 tube (tip) and pale peach or white royal icing. Attach letters.
● Using a no. 3 tube (tip) and pale peach or white royal icing, pipe a small shell border where cakes join board. With a no. 42 tube and the same royal icing, pipe a rope scallop border around sides of cakes, following scribed line. Overpipe with a no. 3 tube. Using a no. 1 tube pipe a fine scalloped line inside scallops.
● Trace remaining letters in each name and inscription; scribe onto board and cakes, taking care to allow for floral spray. With a no. 2 tube (tip) and white icing, pipe a line on back of each plaque 5mm (¼ in) from edge. Reverse each plaque and position them on cake and board, pressing down gently to fix them in place.
● Pipe rest of inscription on cake and board, using a no. 1 tube (tip) and deep peach royal icing as illustrated right. Using a no. 1 tube and pale peach or white icing, pipe ornamental scroll work around lettering on cakes. Pipe a scalloped border at top edges marked with crimper. Pipe a fine scalloped line inside plain scallops.
● Fix floral spray in position, using a little sugarpaste or royal icing to hold stem in place. Attach any additional ornaments in same way, then trim board edge.

OUTLINED FIGURES

*H*uman or animal figures, or objects which are features of a scenic design, can be reproduced as runouts. The Outlined Figure technique is used for a figure or object which requires sharply defined outlines. This type of figure is popular for children's cakes, as it is a way of featuring a favourite cartoon character or hero. If you offer your work for sale, however, take care not to use figures which are trademarked or subject to copyright.

Where several colours are used in the figure, preparing run-icing can be time-consuming, so it is a good idea to prepare multiple drawings and make several runouts at once. The spares can be stored for future use.

Having selected a suitable design, decide on a colour scheme. For outlining you will need a small bag fitted with a no. 1 tube (tip) and filled with royal icing in a dark colour such as brown. List the colours required for flooding and make up a small quantity of run-icing in each shade. Have ready several small paper piping bags; tubes are not really necessary, but the bags must be well made with a sharp point at the end of each. A pencilled initial or two on the outside of each bag will help to identify the colours later.

Step-by-step instructions for outlining and flooding the design are given opposite. The sketch for the figure illustrated is on page 18. The same sketch is used to illustrate the technique of running out a design directly on a cake or plaque, see page 19. Take care not to let the icing overflow the outlines, and use a paintbrush to tease it into any awkward corners. Allow each section to crust over before flooding an adjacent area.

When the figure is complete, and has been allowed to dry, remove the paper and fix the runout to the cake or plaque with a few dots of icing.

~ 1 ~

Fix drawing and wax paper to drying board. It is economical to produce several drawings so that figures can be produced simultaneously. Have ready several bags of run-icing in appropriate colours and one bag of dark royal icing fitted with a no. 1 tube (tip). Using royal icing, outline the sections of the figure.

~ 4 ~

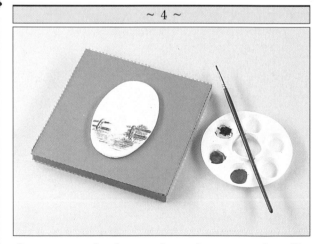

Prepare any background on plaque or cake. For a soft, muted effect, dusting powder (petal dust/ blossom tint) may be used, or background may be piped or painted, as in the illustration above. For more information about painting on plaques, see pages 40-41.

~ 2 ~

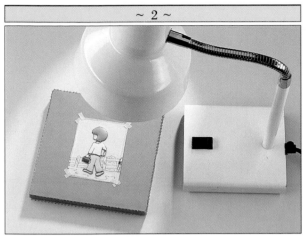

With run-icing, start flooding figure section by section, initially avoiding any adjacent areas. When you have done as much as you can without involving sections that touch each other, place runout under a lamp for a few minutes so that flooded areas crust over.

~ 3 ~

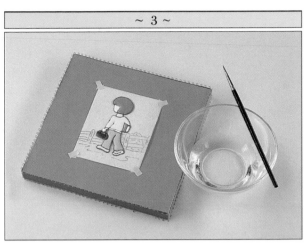

Flood any remaining sections gradually until figure is complete. Leave to dry.

~ 5 ~

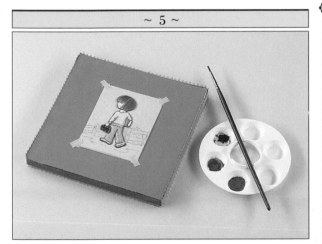

When runout figure is completely dry, paint on any detail. Use a fine sable brush, keeping it as dry as possible; avoid loading it with colour. Dusting powder (petal dust/blossom tint) may be used for shading or highlighting.

~ 6 ~

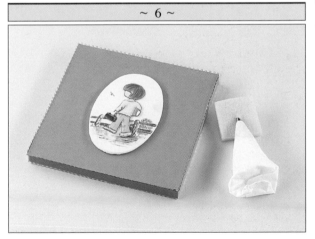

Remove wax paper from runout figure, pipe a few dots on reverse and position it on plaque or cake.

RUNOUTS DIRECT

*T*he technique of running out designs directly on cakes or plaques is useful for runouts which would be difficult to handle on wax paper, such as fragile figures, or those which are composed largely of dark colours, as for the Judo Cake on page 20.

The technique is similar to that used for Outlined Figures on page 16, and uses the same sketch for the purpose of illustration, but for motifs which are to be repeated on sugarpaste-coated surfaces, it may be more convenient to emboss the design rather than to scribe it, see Expert Advice right.

Two important points to remember about running out icing onto sugarpaste instead of wax paper are the necessity to use run-icing of the correct consistency and the need for rapid drying.

This type of work requires slightly thicker run-icing than that used for standard runouts. Follow the recipe on page 8 or use your regular royal icing recipe, but do not thin it too much. Using thicker icing, working fast, and drying the runout rapidly will ensure that the run-icing sets before it has time to dissolve the sugarpaste upon which it has been flooded.

When you are working directly onto a cake, rather than a plaque, avoid using too much heat or leaving the runout under a lamp for too long or the coating on the cake may start to bulge away from the surface.

EXPERT ADVICE

≈

To make an embossing impression for use on sugarpaste-coated surfaces, take a tracing of the figure or motif and place it face down on white paper. Place a piece of perspex (plexiglass) or firm clear plastic over the tracing then, with a no. 1 tube (tip) and royal icing, pipe the outline. Leave the pattern to dry for 24 hours.

Use the embosser by positioning it carefully over the freshly-coated cake or freshly-cut sugarpaste plaque, then press down gently, using even pressure. Take care not to press the edges of the embosser into the paste. Carefully lift the embosser off; leave the paste to dry for at least 24 hours before carrying out further work on it.

You should be able to create several designs before the icing on the embosser begins to disintegrate.

~ 1 ~

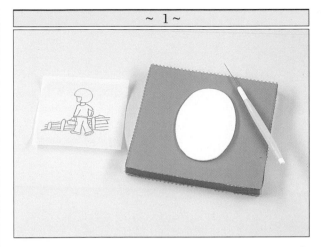

Select a suitable design. This may be entirely composed of runout sections or may comprise a runout on a painted background. Trace picture and scribe outlines on cake or plaque. Alternatively, if working on a sugarpaste-coated surface, emboss design, using technique described under Expert Advice opposite.

~ 2 ~

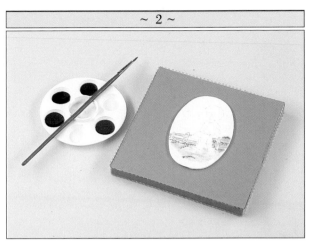

Pipe or paint any background required. If using paint, refer to pages 40-41 for technique. Prepare several bags of run-icing in appropriate colours and one bag of dark royal icing with a no. 1 tube (tip). Ensure that the run-icing is of the correct consistency, see opposite.

~ 3 ~

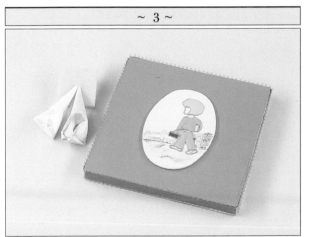

Using royal icing, pipe outline and begin flooding in with run-icing, completing non-adjacent areas first, as for Outlined Figures on pages 16-17.

~ 4 ~

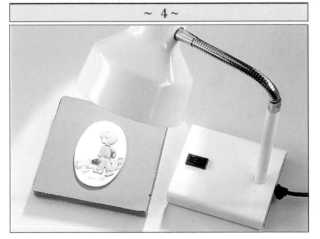

Complete flooding and dry runout quickly.

JUDO CAKE

A strikingly simple design for the judo enthusiast, this cake employs the technique of running out the figure directly onto the cake. Either a firm sponge or a fruit cake would be a suitable base. The design can be adapted to congratulate someone on achieving the next grade; simply pipe on a belt in the appropriate colour.

25 x 20cm (10 x 8 in) cake
apricot glaze
1kg (2 lb) marzipan (almond paste), optional
clear alcohol (gin or vodka), optional
1.25kg (2½ lb) ivory sugarpaste
selection of food colourings
375g (12 oz) Royal Icing for Runouts,
see page 8
EQUIPMENT
30 x 25cm (12 x 10 in) cake board
no. 2 (closed curve) crimper
scriber
No. 1, 2, 3 and 44 piping tubes (tips)
runout equipment, see page 6
1m (1 yd 3 in) red ribbon for cake
1.5m (1¾ yd) ribbon or paper band for board
edge, optional

● If using a fruit cake, cover with apricot glaze, coat with marzipan and brush with alcohol before covering with ivory coloured sugarpaste. A firm sponge or Madeira cake may simply be brushed with apricot glaze and coated with sugarpaste. Crimp a border around top edge of cake. Cover board with sugarpaste, if liked. When paste is dry, attach cake to board.

● Trace judo motif right and scribe or emboss on cake top. Trace inscription, using Eastern alphabet on page 67; scribe on cake. Using a no. 1 tube (tip) and black royal icing, outline judo motif. With run-icing, also black, flood in motif, following step-by-step instructions on pages 18-19. As soon as runout is finished, place it under a lamp to dry.

● With a no. 3 tube (tip) and black royal icing, pipe inscription, varying the pressure in each stroke to create the thin/thick effect which characterises this writing style. Using the same icing, but a no. 1 tube, pipe lines below the motif to indicate the ground. Pipe a rope scroll border at base of cake, using a no. 44 tube and ivory royal icing. Overpipe this in royal icing of the same colour, using a no. 3 tube.

● Using a no. 1 tube (tip) and red royal icing, pipe dots inside crimped edge on top of cake and between scrolls at base, as illustrated opposite. Finish cake sides with a ribbon trim. Trim board edge, if liked, with a ribbon or gold paper band.

SECTIONAL OFF-PIECES

$\mathcal{O}$nce you are confident handling plaques and small runouts your working method can be changed slightly so that you can produce many runouts from a single drawing. This technique is useful for collars made up of sectional runouts where accurate reproduction of six or more identical pieces is required.

Sectional off-pieces have been used for the clouds on the Bon Voyage cake on page 24, but they are more usually employed for top and bottom sectional collars. Many cake decorating books contain patterns suitable for these sectional collars, which have been used on the Anniversary Cake on page 47. Step-by-step instructions for the technique appear opposite.

The method is also suitable for mass producing plaques, models and other ornaments where the pieces are required to be as near identical as possible.

The run-icing for sectional off-pieces should have the same consistency as that discussed under Basic Techniques on page 8; it should hold a trail which disappears when the bowl is gently tapped on the work surface.

EXPERT ADVICE

≈

Colour matching successive batches of icing is not easy; if a design incorporates off-pieces which are the same colour as the cake coating, be sure to make up sufficient icing to coat the cake and make the runouts. For competition work, you may not be able to produce drawings until you know the dimensions of the coated cake. A way around this is to weigh the first batch of icing and count the number of drops of colour used. Make a note of these details and follow them exactly when producing a second batch of icing.

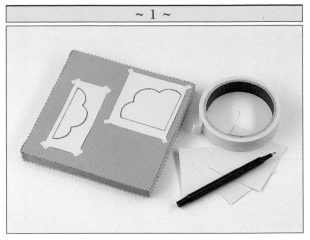

~ 1 ~

The cloud off-pieces described here are used on the Bon Voyage Cake illustrated on page 25. Using cloud templates on page 60, or drawings of your own choice, trace designs. Fix tracings securely to flat surface with either masking tape or drawing pins.

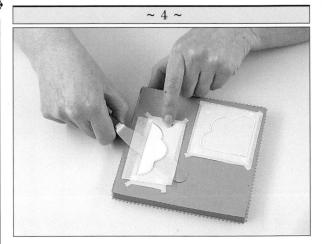

~ 4 ~

Flood the first off-piece with run-icing. Slip a small palette knife under the wax paper. Slide the knife along, vibrating it gently - this will help to level the icing.

~ 2 ~

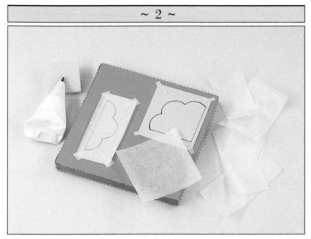

Cut a piece of wax paper for each off-piece required, plus some spares in case of breakages. Pipe small bulbs of icing either onto the drawing or on the reverse of the wax paper. Position the wax paper over the tracing, making sure it lies perfectly flat.

~ 3 ~

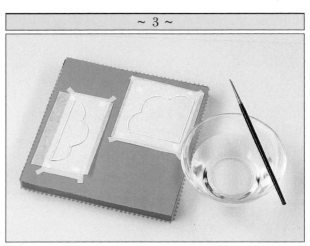

Have ready enough run-icing to flood all the off-pieces, plus a bag of royal icing fitted with a no. 1 tube (tip). Using the royal icing, outline the design as described on page 8, using a damp paintbrush to neaten if necessary.

~ 5 ~

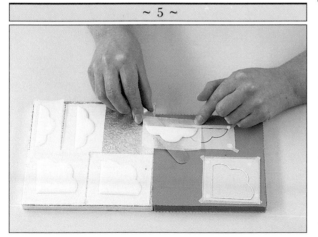

Carefully slide the wax paper onto a drying board. It is important to do this before a crust starts to form on the runout.

~ 6 ~

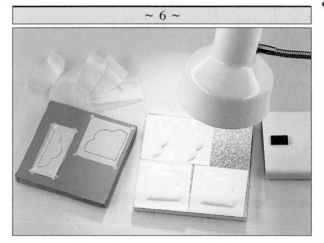

Make another off-piece in exactly the same way, following steps 3-5. Dry complete pieces under an angled desk lamp. When all the off-pieces are dry, pipe on any embellishments required.

BON VOYAGE CAKE

This provides an introduction to sectional off-pieces used as borders wholly attached to the cake surface. Since accurate square edges are required for this design, it is recommended that only royal icing be used for coating. The design is for a 20cm (8 in) square cake; if a larger cake is required, it will be necessary to adjust the size of the templates.

20cm (8 in) square cake
apricot glaze
875g (1¾ lb) marzipan (almond paste)
625g (1¼ lb) royal icing
selection of food colourings
albumen solution for run-icing
E Q U I P M E N T
28cm (11 in) square cake board
runout equipment, see page 6
pair of tweezers
5mm (¼ in) piece of foam
no. 1 and 2 piping tubes (tips)
scriber
about 1.25m (1¼ yd) ribbon or paper band for board edge

● Brush cake with apricot glaze and cover with marzipan. Coat with pale blue royal icing. When final coat is dry, attach cake to board.
● Using templates on page 60, run out 8 large cloud sections, 8 small cloud sections, 2 balloons and 2 baskets, following the step-by-step instructions on pages 22-23. Copy cake opposite or use your own colour scheme for balloons. Trace inscription on page 60 and scribe it on cake top. Trace treetop pattern; scribe on each side of the cake as illustrated opposite.
● Using the tweezers, pick up the piece of foam and dip it into a little green royal icing. 'Paint' treetops on each side of the cake, using a dabbing action to achieve a textured effect. Two or more shades of green look particularly effective.
● Using a no. 2 tube (tip) and white royal icing, pipe a line 5mm (¼ in) from the edge on reverse side of large balloon. Fix piece in place on cake top. Repeat this process with small balloon, baskets and 4 small cloud sections, positioning each piece as illustrated opposite. Fix the large and remaining small cloud sections to the sides of the cake in similar fashion.
● If the cake edges are not quite square and there are gaps where the off-pieces meet, pipe white icing into the gaps and carefully smooth off with a paintbrush or small plastic squeegee.
● Scribe inscription on cake top, then pipe using a no. 1 tube (tip) and white royal icing. Pipe a small shell edge, using a no. 2 tube and pale blue royal icing, between the clouds at the base of the cake where it meets the board. Finally, using a no. 1 tube and brown royal icing, pipe birds on each side of the cake.
● Trim board edge with ribbon or use a silver paper band.

ST PATRICK'S DAY CAKE

*F*ascinating Celtic knotwork and spirals were the inspiration for this design. It can easily be adapted for Scottish, Welsh, Cornish or Breton saints or occasions, provided the inscriptions and side designs are changed.

18cm (7 in) square cake
apricot glaze
750g (1½ lb) marzipan (almond paste)
875g (1 ¾ lb) royal icing
selection of food colourings
albumen solution for run-icing
E Q U I P M E N T
25cm (10 in) square cake board
runout equipment, see page 6
scriber
no. 1, 2 and 3 piping tubes (tips)
about 1m (1 yd 3 in) ribbon or paper band for board edge

● Brush cake with apricot glaze and cover with marzipan. Coat cake and board with pale green royal icing. When final coat is dry, attach cake to board.
● Using templates on page 59, run out 4 border sections, 4 shields and 4 harps following the step-by-step instructions for sectional off-pieces on pages 22-23. Trace and make 4 single shamrocks, using figure piping technique, see pages 28-29.
● Trace inscription on page 58 and make runout letters, following technique described on page 13. Trace template for board runout on page 59; scribe outline on coated board. Trace shamrock design on same page; scribe on cake sides as illustrated opposite. Using a no. 1 tube (tip) and green royal icing, pipe shamrocks, using tiny heart shapes for leaves.
● When harps are dry, paint them with gold colouring. Leave to dry, then fix harps to shields, using a few dots of icing. Fix shields to cake sides

by piping a line of green royal icing with a no. 2 tube (tip), 5mm (¼ in) from edges on reverse of each shield, then pressing shields gently against the cake.
● Runout bottom border directly on board, following instructions on page 50. Pipe a small shell border at base of cake, where it meets board runout, using a no. 3 tube (tip) and pale green royal icing. Outline board runout using a no. 1 tube and green royal icing.
● With a no. 1 tube (tip) and pale green royal icing, pipe a few dots on reverse of runout letters and fix them in position on top of cake. Using a no. 2 tube and pale green icing, pipe a line along one side just inside the cake rim. Carefully position one of the runout top border pieces over this to fix it to cake top. Repeat process with remaining 3 border sections.
● Finish cake by piping a scalloped line along inner edge of top border pieces as illustrated right, using green royal icing and a no. 1 tube (tip). Pipe a small bulb of icing on each top corner and position runout shamrocks. Trim board edge with ribbon or paper band.

EXPERT ADVICE
≈
Cutting lots of pieces of masking tape for fixing designs and wax paper for runouts can be tedious. A quick way to do this is to tape a length of masking tape on a ceramic tile and cut it into handy lengths, using a craft knife or scalpel. Each piece of tape can then be peeled off, using the knife, as required.

FIGURE PIPING

$\mathcal{L}$ike the technique for Outlined Figures on page 16, figure piping is used to produce figures or objects and is ideal for the reproduction of badges or coats of arms. No dark outline is used, so the figures have a softer appearance. They also have more depth because certain areas are built up to give an effect reminiscent of half relief. They are not to be confused with freehand piped figures, which display even greater relief. The consistency of the icing for these figures needs to be almost that of soft peak: if you put a small sample on the work surface and brush it to a long point with a paintbrush, the icing should stay put but lose the marks of the brush. As with all runout work, the icing should be coloured, if required, before being thinned to the correct consistency. No piping tubes (tips) are required; very small bags made with a sharp point will serve well, see Outlined Figures, page 16.

The preparation of the icing can be time-consuming, so it is sensible to produce several figures at a time, working on one while another is drying. Keep one original drawing spare for reference. Look closely at the original drawing and note on it the order in which you will work - a sort of 'Icing by Numbers', see step 2 opposite. The method for preparing the icing is the same as that for Outlined Figures on page 16, the important difference being the consistency of the icing. The figures described opposite are used on Santa's Slide, illustrated on page 31. Templates for the penguins or Santa are on page 30.

EXPERT ADVICE

≈

When you are flooding a layer of icing on top of a previous layer dried under a lamp, always allow the first layer to cool before covering it. If you fail to do this, the second layer will dry on contact with the first and you will not have time to smooth it out.

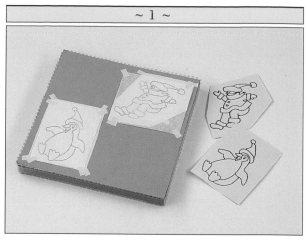

~ 1 ~

Prepare several drawings and tape or pin a piece of wax paper over each one. It is important not to move the paper once work commences. Keep your original drawing handy as it may be needed for reference. Have ready several bags of runicing in appropriate colours, making sure that it is of the correct consistency, see left.

~ 4 ~

Some areas can be given a textured effect, either by stippling the surface with icing and a paintbrush once the figure has dried or by using icing of full piping consistency, as for Santa's beard and the fur trim on his suit.

~ 2 ~

Start with those parts of the figure that appear to be furthest away. No outlining is necessary; simply push the icing to the shape required or use a paintbrush to tease it into position. Parts like Santa's tummy, which need to be emphasised, can have a bulb of icing piped first to help accentuate the shape.

~ 3 ~

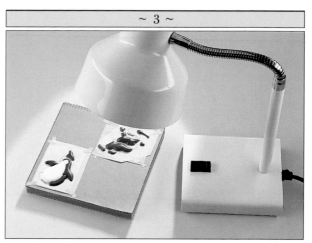

When bulbs have crusted over, pipe a second layer on top. Continue flooding other areas, always working from background to foreground but avoiding areas adjacent to each other. Very dark colours should be allowed to dry completely before paler icing is piped next to them.

~ 5 ~

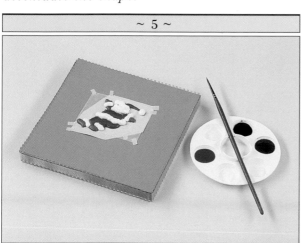

When each figure has dried, paint or pipe on any fine details. Allow to dry completely, then store figures carefully or use immediately.

~ 6 ~

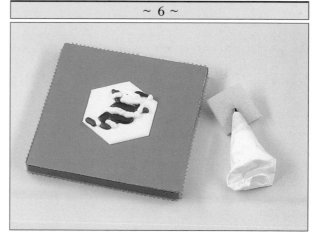

To fix a figure to a cake or plaque, turn it face down onto a piece of foam, peel off the backing paper, pipe some small bulbs of icing on the reverse, then carefully attach it where required.

SANTA'S SLIDE

$\mathcal{A}$ny square sponge or fruit cake would be suitable for this design. Step-by-step instructions for making the runout figures for the slide are on pages 28-29.

15cm (6 in) square cake, 5cm (2 in) deep
apricot glaze
750g (1½ lb) marzipan (almond paste)
albumen solution for run-icing
caster (superfine) sugar
selection of food colourings
E Q U I P M E N T
25 x 20cm (10 x 8 in) cake board
runout equipment, see page 6
no. 2 and 1 piping tubes (tips)
about 1m (1 yd 3 in) ribbon or paper band for
board edge

● Cut cake in half diagonally to form 2 triangles. Sandwich pieces together, using apricot glaze or marzipan (almond paste), so that when stood on end, the cake forms a ramp shape as illustrated opposite. Brush cake with apricot glaze and cover with marzipan (almond paste). Using white royal icing, flat ice the sloping side; rough ice the remaining sides to simulate snow, see Expert Advice. Coat the cake board with white royal icing. When icing is dry, attach cake to board.
● Using templates right and following step-by-step instructions on pages 28-29, make figures. When dry, pipe a line down the reverse side of each figure, using a no. 2 tube (tip) and white royal icing. Carefully position figures on cake.
● Trace 'Happy Christmas' inscription on page 61 and scribe on cake board. Pipe lettering and exclamation mark, first using a no. 2 tube (tip) and white icing, then overpiping in red with a no. 1 tube. Trim board edge and complete scene with Christmas ornaments.

> **EXPERT ADVICE**
> ≈
> To enhance snow effect on sides of cake, let flat icing dry before adding rough icing. Sprinkle caster (superfine) sugar over freshly rough-iced sides, dusting off any excess sugar after icing has dried.

EASTER CAKE

A colourful bunch of flowers is one of the most useful runout patterns, suitable for almost any shape, size of cake or occasion. Simply by changing the inscription on the label, this tulip design can be adapted for birthdays, anniversaries, good luck or get well cakes. Keep the rest of the decoration simple and let the bouquet speak for itself.

25 x 20cm (10 x 8 in) oval sponge cake filled with jam and buttercream
apricot glaze
315g (10 oz) ivory-coloured sugarpaste
250g (8 oz) Royal Icing for Runouts,
see page 8
selection of food colourings
E Q U I P M E N T
20 x 25cm (12 x 10 in) cake board
runout equipment, see page 6
no 1, 3, 44 and 2 piping tubes (tips)
0.9m (1 yd) x 7.5cm (3 in) deep gold paper band
1.25m (1¼ yd) green ribbon

● Brush top of cake with apricot glaze and coat with ivory sugarpaste, smoothing surface. Attach cake to board.
● Using template on page 58 and figure piping technique described on pages 28-29, make runout bunch of tulips and label. Use colour scheme of own choice or follow illustration opposite. When dry, pipe inscription on label using a no. 1 tube (tip) and brown royal icing. With the same tube, pipe cord attaching label to flower stems. When inscription is dry, pipe a line on the back of the bouquet, 5mm (¼ in) from the edge, using a no. 3 tube and ivory-tinted royal icing. Place runout on cake top, allowing it to stand slightly proud of sugarpaste surface.
● Using a no. 44 tube (tip) and ivory royal icing, pipe a simple shell border around top edge of cake. With a no. 2 tube and icing of same colour, pipe two rows of linework inside border, then overpipe first line. With a no. 1 tube and brown royal icing, pipe a small dot inside the linework at each join in the pattern, as illustrated opposite.
● Complete cake with a band of gold paper and a ribbon around the sides.

EXPERT ADVICE

≈

The glossy surface of a runout is easily marked. Try not to touch the top of the runout with the fingers; handle it like a photographic negative. When fixing a runout to a cake surface, try to settle it in position with the back of a finger rather than by using the fingertips.

DAD'S BIRTHDAY CAKE

Chrysanthemums are one of the flowers considered to be suitable for 'masculine' cakes. Here, classical Chinese embroidery patterns have been adapted for runout corner pieces.

18cm (7 in) square cake
apricot glaze
750g (1½ lb) marzipan (almond paste)
clear alcohol (gin or vodka)
875g (1 ¾ lb) ivory-coloured sugarpaste
250g (8 oz) Royal Icing for Runouts,
see page 8
selection of food colourings
dusting powder (petal dust/blossom tint),
optional
E Q U I P M E N T
25cm (10 in) square cake board
floral embossing tools, optional
runout equipment, see page 6
airbrush, optional
scriber
no. 2, 1 and 3 piping tubes (tips)
1m (1 yd 3 in) ribbon or paper band
for board edge

● Brush cake with apricot glaze and cover with marzipan (almond paste). Brush with alcohol and cover with ivory sugarpaste, smoothing top and sides. Emboss simple flower sprays on cake sides or, when coating is dry, pipe freehand embroidery flowers on sides. Use remaining sugarpaste to cover board, embossing it or embroidering it to match the cake. When dry, centre cake on coated board, attaching it with royal icing.
● Using templates on page 61, runout 2 each of chrysanthemum corner pieces, following figure piping technique described in step-by-step instructions on pages 28-29. Make runout letters for DAD, using template on page 61 and technique described on page 13. When lettering is dry,

shade bottom half of each letter, using an airbrush, see Expert Advice, or by brushing with dusting powder (petal dust/blossom tint.)
● Trace 'Happy Birthday' inscription on page 61 and scribe on cake top as illustrated right. Pipe inscription using a no. 2 tube (tip) and ivory royal icing, then overpipe using a no. 1 tube and rust-tinted royal icing. Fix runout lettering in place, using a few dots of ivory icing. If embossed flower sprays have been used on board, overpipe them with a no. 1 tube and rust royal icing. Similarly, overpipe embossed sprays on side of cake, using ivory royal icing.
● Pipe a border of bulbs along base of cake, using ivory royal icing and a no. 3 tube (tip). Overpipe, using the same tube. On the top edge, pipe a line 4.5cm (1¾ in) either side of one of the corners, using ivory royal icing and a no. 3 tube. Carefully position one of the corner pieces over the piped line, so that the leaves extend over the edge; gently press it into place. Position a matching corner piece in the diagonally opposite corner, then attach the remaining pieces.
● Pipe tiny embroidery dots, resembling fern leaves, on the top edge between the runouts, using a no. 1 tube (tip) and ivory royal icing. Trim board edge.

EXPERT ADVICE

≈

Spraying small items, like individual letters, with an airbrush can be tricky, since the air flow can be strong enough to blow the item away. If you use this method of shading, be sure to stick each piece of wax paper down firmly first.

MODELS & DOUBLE-SIDED RUNOUTS

*A*s a form of prefabricated decoration, runouts lend themselves readily to the making of large and small models. Step-by-step instructions for making two perennially popular models - a cradle and a heart - are given opposite. These are used on the finished cakes on pages 38 and 52.

Highly accurate working drawings are required for this type of work. Piping must be equally precise; otherwise there could be problems with fitting the pieces together. Small models can be assembled using royal icing of piping consistency, but larger pieces may need internal supports. These can be made of sugar cubes cemented together with royal icing, or of gum paste. They should not be visible when the model has been assembled.

The technique for making the model will depend upon the effect you wish to create: the basic runout method described on page 8 is suitable for a smooth design, whereas a textured pattern such as a tiled roof may be achieved more readily by using the outlined figure technique described on pages 16-17.

Ornaments which are designed to stand up on a cake will have a more professional appearance if they are made double sided. One way of doing this is to make two runouts of the same design, one a mirror image of the other, sticking them together when dry, but this method tends to emphasise any little inaccuracies in the piped outline. Turning the runout over and repeating the flooding on the reverse, although more difficult, gives a better finish.

The problems are similar to those encountered when piping runouts directly onto a cake or plaque: the second runout, if not dried rapidly and thoroughly, can cause the underlying sugar surface to dissolve, leading to the formation of pits and hollows. Using run-icing similar in consistency to that required for Figure Piping, see pages 28-29, will help, as will quick drying.

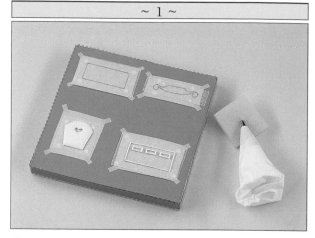

~ 1 ~

SINGLE-SIDED RUNOUT (CRADLE) *Using templates on page 65, trace plaque and parts for cradle, making 2 each of sides and ends and 4 rocker pieces. Fix drawings and wax paper as on pages 22-23. Using basic technique, outline and flood all sections. On areas where icing may over-run, overpipe lines before flooding.*

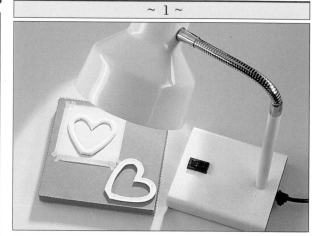

~ 1 ~

DOUBLE-SIDED RUNOUT (HEART) *Prepare heart-shaped plaque, using template on page 57. Set aside. Trace heart ornament on same page. Fix drawing and wax paper as described on pages 22-23. Following step-by-step instructions on pages 10-11, outline and flood runout. When thoroughly dry, remove wax paper and carefully turn the runout over.*

~ 2 ~

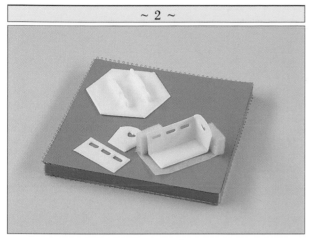

When all sections are dry, remove them from wax paper. Join rocker pieces in pairs back-to-back; when dry, fix to plaque. Assemble cradle from base up, using no. 1 tube (tip) and icing of piping consistency to join pieces, and supporting sections with bits of foam or plastic bricks until completely dry.

~ 3 ~

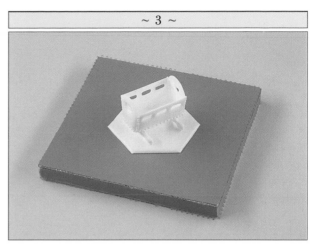

Attach cradle to rockers. Overpipe joins, if necessary, with small shells. Use on Christening Cake, illustrated on page 39, or on cake of your own design.

~ 2 ~

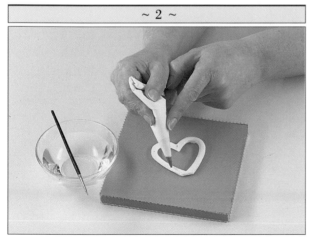

Using icing of same consistency as for figure piping, see pages 28-29, quickly flood back of runout. Set to dry immediately, leaving runout under a lamp for 2-3 hours. Where appropriate, disguise join and decorate edge of runout with microdots, see page 13.

~ 3 ~

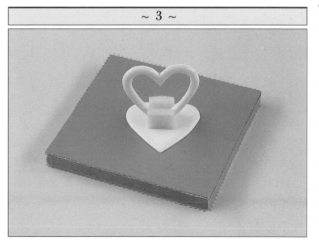

Attach ornament to runout plaque, using icing of piping consistency and a no. 1 tube (tip). Support with piece of foam until dry. Disguise icing 'cement' with a floral spray. Use on Valentine's Day Cake, illustrated on page 53, or on cake of your own design.

CHRISTENING CAKE

The basic design for this cake can be adapted for any occasion simply by changing the ornament and inscription. A fruit or sponge cake may be used. Step-by-step instructions for making the cradle are on pages 36-37.

25 x 20cm (10 x 8 in) oval cake
apricot glaze
1.25kg (2½ lb) marzipan (almond paste),
optional
clear alcohol (gin or vodka)
1.5kg (3 lb) white sugarpaste
125g (4 oz) Royal Icing for Runouts,
see page 8
12 large, 36 medium and 36 small sugarpaste
blossoms
selection of food colourings
E Q U I P M E N T
30 x 25cm (12 x 10 in) oval cake board
crimpers or embossers, optional
Garrett frill cutter
runout equipment, see page 6
scriber
no. 3, 2 and 1 piping tubes (tips)
cocktail stick (toothpick)
1.25m (1¼ yd) ribbon or silver paper band for
board edge

● If using a fruit cake, cover with apricot glaze, coat with marzipan and brush with alcohol before covering with white sugarpaste. A sponge cake may simply be brushed with apricot glaze and coated with sugarpaste. Use some of the remaining sugarpaste to coat cake board, crimping a design around edge, if liked. Reserve enough sugarpaste to make Garrett frills for side of cake.

● Following the step-by-step instructions on pages 36-37, and using the templates on page 65, make the runout cradle and assemble it on the plaque.

● The side of the cake is decorated with Garrett frills. Measure height and circumference of cake and make a greaseproof paper (parchment) template. Fold template into 6 equal sections and cut the top of each section to a scallop shape. Scribe scallops onto cake sides. Trace template on page 58 for piped embroidery at top of scallops; scribe onto cake, see illustration right. With a no. 3 tube (tip) and white royal icing, pipe a small shell border around base of cake. Using the cutter, reserved white sugarpaste and cocktail stick (toothpick), make a double layer of Garrett frills for side of cake (see Note).

● Moisten marked scallops on cake with a damp brush and quickly attach frills, gently lifting them with a soft dry brush to create a delicate effect. Neaten top edge of each frill with a picot edging piped with a no. 1 tube (tip) and white royal icing.

● Using a no. 1 tube (tip) and pink royal icing, pipe embroidery at top of scallops. Fix plaque with cradle to top of cake, using a no. 2 tube and white royal icing.

● Trace baby's name, using alphabet on page 68. Scribe name on cake, then pipe lettering, using a no. 1 tube (tip) and pink royal icing. Fix blossoms around cradle and on embroidery at top of scallops, using a no. 1 tube and white royal icing. Using dark pink royal icing and a no. 1 tube, pipe a centre into each blossom. Trim board edge with ribbon or a silver paper band.

NOTE Detailed instructions for making the Garrett frills are not included in this book as the technique is covered elsewhere in the *Sugarcraft Skills Series*.

PAINTING ON RUNOUT PLAQUES

*T*he technique for applying food colourings to runouts is the same for an eyebrow as for an entire scene, although the latter demands considerably more artistry and expertise. The important point to bear in mind is that the surface on which you are working is highly absorbent, so your paintbrush must always be kept as dry as possible.

EQUIPMENT
non-toxic pencil
small palette
selection of food colourings
superwhite powder
small quantity of clear alcohol (gin or vodka)
fine sable brushes, no. 2, 1, and 000

Step-by-step instructions for painting on a runout are given opposite. The plaque described is used on the Child's Birthday Cake which is illustrated on page 43.

It is a good idea to begin with a simple design in two or three colours, progressing to more complicated scenes as the technique is mastered.

Use paler colours first; they can always be darkened or shaded, but it is very difficult to correct colours that are too dark. Mix colours on a palette. Any type of food colouring can be used, but pastes and powders should be thinned with a little alcohol rather than water as the alcohol will evaporate more quickly and the runout will therefore dry more efficiently. Superwhite powder can be mixed with colours to provide tints; it also produces a matt finish similar to poster paint.

Sable brushes are best for this work as they hold the colour until you release it by pressing the brush onto a surface. Wash brushes in water and keep a damp cloth handy to wipe them on.

~ 1 ~

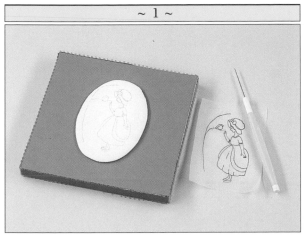

Have ready a 7 x 10.5cm (2¾ x 4¼ in) oval runout plaque. Trace illustration opposite or use picture of your own choice. Place tracing face down; trace over outlines, using non-toxic pencil. Position tracing on plaque. Go over lines again, to transfer picture, using a pencil rather than a scriber to avoid damaging surface.

~ 2 ~

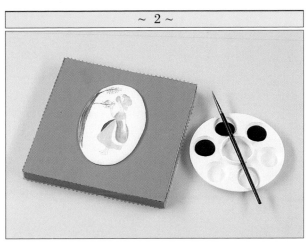

Paint in background areas, using palest tints. When foreground is added, stronger colours can be used to give greater definition and dimension.

~ 3 ~

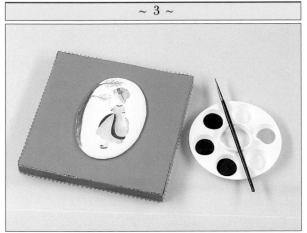

Add shading and details gradually. If picture you are copying does not show shading, imagine which side the light source illuminates; shade on opposite side.

~ 4 ~

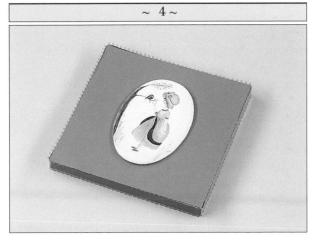

Finish with highlights. If any areas require more definition, outline them with grey or coffee colouring, applied with a fine brush.

CHILD'S BIRTHDAY CAKE

Children love to save keepsakes from their birthday cakes - a painted plaque will be especially popular because it can be eaten later! Step-by-step instructions for making the plaque are on page 41. It can be prepared well in advance and the cake decorated simply and swiftly a day or so before the party. The simpler the cake, the better the plaque will stand out as a feature.

25 x 20cm (10 x 8 in) oval sponge cake
apricot glaze
1.25kg (2½ lb) white sugarpaste
375g (12 oz) Royal Icing for Runouts,
see page 8
selection of food colourings
EQUIPMENT
30 x 25cm (12 x 10 in) oval cake board
painted plaque, see pages 40-41
runout equipment, see page 6
no. 2 (closed curve) crimper, optional
no. 1, 2, 3 and 44 piping tubes (tips)
about 1.25m (1¼ yd) narrow brown ribbon for
side of cake
about 0.9m (1 yd) ribbon or paper band for
board edge

● Brush cake with apricot glaze and cover with sugarpaste, smoothing top and sides. Use remaining sugarpaste to cover board, scalloping and crimping edge if liked. Allow to dry, then attach cake to coated board with royal icing.
● Have ready painted plaque, using design on page 40 or illustration of your own choice. Using two colours of royal icing in a single bag fitted with a no. 44 tube (tip), pipe a rope scroll around base of cake. Trace a suitable inscription, using alphabet on page 68; scribe on cake top. Pipe lettering for inscription, using a no. 2 tube and white royal icing, then overpipe using a no. 1 tube and yellow royal icing.

● Working on reverse side of dry plaque, pipe a line of icing 5mm (¼ in) inside edge, using a no. 2 tube (tip) and white royal icing. Turn plaque over, position it on cake, and press it gently onto surface. Pipe scalloped linework around plaque, using a no. 1 tube and white royal icing.
● Pipe a top border of simple shells, using a no. 44 tube (tip) and white royal icing. Using icing of the same colour, overpipe each side of border with a no. 3 tube. Tie the ribbon around the cake and trim board with ribbon or a gold paper band.

COMING OF AGE CAKE

*C*lever use of runout lettering gives the illusion of a runout collar in a design which can be adapted for other occasions. Step-by-step instructions for making the curved runout figures on the side of the cake are on page 46.

20cm (8 in) round cake
apricot glaze
1.25kg (2½ lb) marzipan (almond paste)
875g (1¾ lb) royal icing
albumen solution for run-icing
selection of food colourings
E Q U I P M E N T
25cm (10 in) round cake board
runout equipment, see page 6
no. 3, 2 and 1 piping tubes (tips)
about 0.9m (1 yd) ribbon or paper band for
board edge

● Brush cake with apricot glaze and cover with marzipan (almond paste). Coat cake and board with royal icing. When final coat is dry, attach cake to board.

● Using technique described on page 13 and alphabet on page 69, make runout letters to spell CONGRATULATIONS and appropriate name. Outline letters in dark blue royal icing, and flood them with run-icing in a paler shade.

● Make a double-sided runout figure 18 and plaque, using templates on page 57 and technique described on pages 36–37. Run out 6 dark blue sports figures, using templates on page 65. Dry them on a curve which matches curve on cake sides, following technique described on page 46.

● Pipe a border of bulbs around base of cake, using white royal icing and no. 3 tube (tip). Pipe two rows of linework on coated board, outlining pairs of bulbs in bottom corner, using white royal icing and a no. 2 tube, followed by no. 1 tube. Pipe a small S- and C- scroll edge to linework, using a no. 1 tube and blue royal icing.

● When dry, attach sports figures by piping two or three small bulbs of icing on reverse of each figure before carefully positioning them on cake side. With a no. 1 tube (tip) and white royal icing, pipe a few lines underneath each figure to suggest the ground. Pipe ski pole using royal icing of same colour as runouts.

● Trace oval template on page 65 and scribe on centre of top of cake as guide for linework. Pipe with white royal icing and no. 2 and no. 1 tubes (tips). Finish linework with a line of small S- and C- scrolls in blue royal icing with a no. 1 tube.

● Make a greaseproof paper (parchment) template of the cake top. With a pencil and ruler, divide circle neatly into quarters. Arrange dried runout letters on paper so that they are evenly spaced around circumference, each letter half inside and half outside the circle. Mark position of each letter on paper, then, using paper as a guide, transfer letters to cake top, attaching them with a couple of small bulbs of icing piped on the bottom half of underside of each letter in 'Congratulations' and the top half of each letter in the name.

● Using a no. 1 tube (tip) and white royal icing, pipe a tiny shell border on top edge of cake between inscriptions and around top edge of cake board. Finish cake by positioning figure 18 plaque, using a little icing to fix it in place. Trim board edge with ribbon or silver paper band.

NOTE The templates on page 57 include suitable numerals for a 21st birthday cake.

DRYING RUNOUTS ON A CURVE

Flat figures and plaques are ideal for square, hexagonal and other angled shapes, but they can look incongruous on curved surfaces, such as the Coming of Age cake on the previous page. Once mastered, the ability to create curved runouts can lead the cake decorator into the area of developing runout petals for waterlilies and fantasy flowers, and into creating more adventurous models.

For curved runouts on cakes, what is needed is a drying surface which replicates the curve on the coated cake. For ornaments, the required curve, whether concave or convex, will be dictated by the design. Many items may be used as curved drying surfaces. Examples include polystyrene dummies or sections, plastic tubing or guttering, cardboard tubes and cake tins (pans), see Expert Advice.

The consistency of the run-icing should be fractionally thicker than that required for Figure Piping, see pages 28-29. If the icing is too thin, it will run down the curve before it dries.

Speed is essential both while running out the plaque or figure and when drying it.

EXPERT ADVICE

≈

When making curved runouts for use on the side of a cake, be wary of using the tin (pan) in which the cake was baked as a drying surface; remember that the marzipan (almond paste) and sugarpaste or royal icing will have altered the dimensions of the cake.

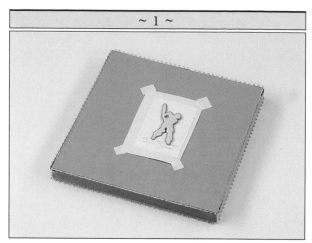

1

Prepare run-icing of the correct consistency, see left. Trace selected design. The illustration above shows one of the runout sports figures used on the Coming of Age cake illustrated on page 45. Fix wax paper over drawing with a few bulbs of icing. Pipe outline in royal icing, then flood in, see Note below.

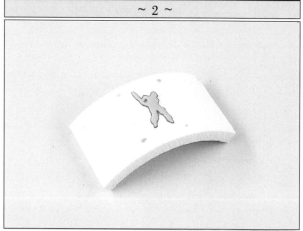

2

Free wax paper by sliding a palette knife between it and the drawing. Position runout on curved drying surface. Dry quickly. Take care that identical pieces are all dried at the same angle on the curve.

NOTE *When working with two or more colours, fix drawing and wax paper to curved drying surface and work directly on that.*

ANNIVERSARY CAKE

Illustrated on page 49

*O*verlays are useful fillers between sections of runout borders. They can take many forms - simple geometric or floral shapes, hearts and butterflies being popular. Here the wheel of the flower barrow is echoed in the circular overlays decorated with blossoms which embellish the top border of the cake.

18cm (7 in) round cake
apricot glaze
1.25kg (2½ lb) marzipan (almond paste)
875g (1¾ lb) royal icing
albumen solution for run-icing
selection of food colourings including dusting
powder (petal dust/blossom tints)
assorted tiny sugarpaste blossoms
E Q U I P M E N T
25cm (10 in) round cake board
runout equipment, see page 6
no 2, 1 and 3 piping tubes (tips)
about 0.9m (1 yd) ribbon or paper band for
board edge

● Brush cake with apricot glaze and cover with marzipan (almond paste). Coat cake with royal icing. When final coat of icing is dry, attach cake to board.
● Using templates on page 62, make 6 runout top collar sections, 6 runout board collar sections and 6 runout overlay circles, following the step-by-step instructions for Sectional Off-Pieces on pages 22-23.
● Following basic technique described on pages 8-9, make runout base for flower barrow in ivory run-icing and one plant pot in terracotta run-icing. Make barrow wheel by first piping outlines of circles; make spokes by piping from centre point to inner circle, taking line of icing over edge of inner circle; pipe curved line joining spokes, then flood in outer circle. Using a no. 2 tube (tip)

and ivory royal icing, pipe the curved barrow handle on wax paper.
● When collar sections are dry, pipe microdot embellishment, see page 13. When flower barrow is dry, shade it with dusting powder (petal dust/blossom tint) if liked.
● Measure height and circumference of cake and make a greaseproof paper (parchment) template for sides. Fold template into 6 equal sections. Trace pattern for side linework, see page 62, on each section, keeping patterns evenly spaced and level. Scribe on cake side, then pipe, using ivory royal icing and no. 2 and 1 tubes (tips).
● Trace inscription and scribe it onto cake top; pipe it, using a no. 1 tube (tip) and terracotta royal icing. Using dusting powder, colour in background on cake top.

Continued on page 48

Continued from page 47

● Reverse flower barrow runout. Using a no. 3 tube (tip) and ivory royal icing, pipe a line in position shown by broken line on barrow template. Allow line to set, then overpipe with same tube. Position barrow at an angle on cake top. With a no. 1 tube and ivory icing, fix barrow handle in position, using small dots of icing. Pipe a small bulb of icing on back of plant pot and fix in position on cake top as illustrated opposite.

● Using small dots of icing, fix tiny sugarpaste blossoms in place in barrow and plant pot, reserving some blossoms for base and circular overlays. Pipe tiny green leaves among blossoms, using a small piping bag cut to a 'V' at the end. Add some green dots - piped with a no. 1 tube (tip) - to suggest fern-type foliage. The sketch on page 47 illustrates the completed barrow and flower-filled plant pot.

● Reverse runout board collar sections. Positioning one at a time, pipe a line 5mm (¼ in) from inside edge, using ivory royal icing and a no. 2 tube (tip), then place section right way up on board, ensuring that it matches side linework. Using a no. 2 tube (tip) and ivory royal icing, pipe small shells between base of cake and runout sections.

● Using a no. 1 tube (tip) and ivory royal icing, fix small sprays of blossoms at joins between runout sections. Pipe foliage between flowers, as for barrow on cake top, and between sprays and board edge.

● Fix top runout collar sections onto cake by piping a line of ivory royal icing with a no. 2 tube (tip) just inside edge on one sixth of cake top. Make sure line matches position of base runouts. Position one collar section over line and gently press into place. Fix remaining sections in the same way.

● Neaten underside of runout sections by piping a row of small shells, using a no. 2 tube (tip) and ivory royal icing, in angle where runout joins the cake side.

● Attach some tiny blossoms to circular runout overlays, using a no. 1 tube and ivory royal icing.

Position overlays between top runout sections, attaching them with a few dots of ivory icing. Using no 2 and 1 tubes and ivory icing, pipe two rows of linework inside top runout sections.

● Trim the board edge with ribbon or gold paper band.

EXPERT ADVICE

≈

Streakiness in runouts can be caused by different consistencies in the same bag of royal icing. When the bag of icing is resting with its tip in a damp cloth or sponge, the icing nearest the tip absorbs moisture and so its consistency is altered. Always squeeze out and discard a little icing when the bag has been resting and you will avoid this problem.

FULL COLLARS

*P*art of the classical English style of cake decorating for most of this century, full collars were once frequently seen on commercial celebration cakes. Today they are more often seen on exhibition work. Solid collars are the easiest for beginners to attempt, but with a little practice, expertise in making and handling collars with open sections will come.

Full collars are usually designed to extend over the outer rim of the cake top. They can also be used to create a frame for a cake top scene; in this instance the collar may fit entirely within the cake top and the border may take the form of a simple piped edge directly on the cake.

There are several ways of removing the collar from the wax paper and transferring it to the cake. One method is to place the dried collar on a turntable or work surface with a small section extending over the edge. Start peeling wax paper off runout by pulling it downwards. Rotate collar slightly and repeat until entire collar is free. Alternatively, slide a taut piece of thread or thin palette knife between collar and paper. This works best when there is no dot edging to collar.

RUNOUTS ONTO A COATED CAKE BOARD

Running out a bottom collar directly on the cake board saves having to handle a second full collar. This is relatively easy on uncoated boards, but a special technique is required for coated boards. Using royal icing, pipe the outline of the collar onto the board. Prepare two or three bags of run-icing and use one of them to flood an area about 5cm (2 in) wide between the cake edge and the piped outline. Continue flooding section by section on alternate sides, as shown in step 3 opposite. Follow the rules for flooding onto sugar as described in Runouts Direct on pages 18-19: use icing of the correct consistency, work quickly and dry rapidly.

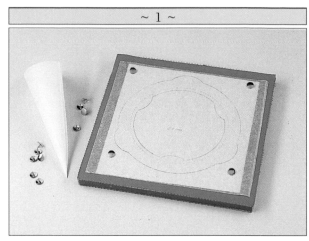

~ 1 ~

Trace design. Fix drawing and wax paper firmly, making sure both are perfectly flat. Have ready several bags of run-icing and one bag of royal icing fitted with a no. 1 tube (tip). It is important to ensure that you have sufficient run-icing to finish flooding the collar once you have started work.

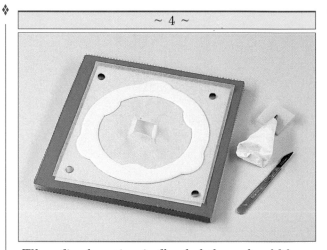

~ 4 ~

When final section is flooded there should be no visible join in collar. Cut a cross in the centre of the wax paper with a scalpel; this will help to release tension as icing dries and prevent collar from cracking. Microdots or other edging may be piped when collar has dried, see page 13.

~ 2 ~

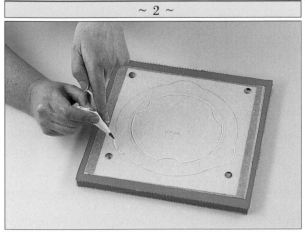

Using royal icing, outline design. Follow basic technique for runouts described on page 8, piping inside edge first. Ensure that any joins are neat.

~ 3 ~

Flood collar in 5cm (2 in) sections, using a paintbrush if necessary to tease icing into corners. Having completed first section, flood section to its left. Then flood a section to right of first section. Continue flooding collar design in this fashion, working on alternate areas on either side of the starter section.

~ 5 ~

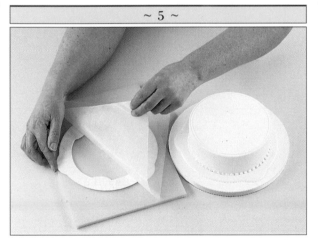

Remove wax paper by inverting collar onto block of foam and peeling it off, or by using one of the other methods described opposite. Take care never to touch upper surface of runout because fingermarks will show. To attach collar to cake, pipe a circle of icing just inside top rim on cake top, using a no. 2 tube (tip) and royal icing. Position collar on this.

~ 6 ~

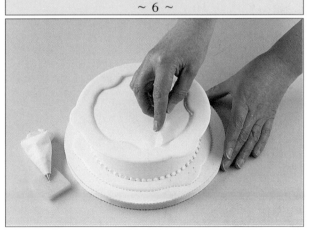

Neaten inner edge by piping royal icing into any gaps and smoothing with a damp paintbrush or plastic squeegee. Finish underside of collar by piping small shells with a no. 2 tube (tip) in angle where collar meets cake side. It may be necessary to work with cake at eye level to do this.

VALENTINE'S DAY CAKE

*M*ore advanced runout skills are employed in this romantic design. Step-by-step instructions for making the double-sided heart ornament are on page 36-37.

20cm (8 in) heart-shaped cake
apricot glaze
875g (1¾ lb) marzipan (almond paste)
625g (1¼ lb) royal icing
selection of food colourings
about 30 sugar or silk roses
E Q U I P M E N T
28cm (11 in) heart-shaped cake board
runout equipment, see page 6
scriber
no. 1, 3 and 2 piping tubes (tips)
1m (1 yd 3 in) ribbon or paper band for
board edge

● Brush cake with apricot glaze and cover with marzipan (almond paste). Coat cake and board with pale pink royal icing. When final coat is dry, attach cake to board. Using template on page 63 and the step-by-step instructions on pages 50-51, make a full collar top runout with marble effect, see Expert Advice. Make a double-sided ornament, as described on pages 36-37. Repeat marble effect used in top collar.

● Make a greaseproof paper (parchment) template for side of cake, and fold into 6 equal sections. Trace side design on page 63 in each section; scribe on cake side. Pipe design as illustrated right, using a no.3 tube (tip) and pale pink royal icing. Overpipe with a no. 2, then with a no. 1 tube.

● Using a no. 1 tube (tip) and pink royal icing, pipe a line 2cm (¾ in) inside edge of cake board. With pale pink run-icing, flood in the area of the board surrounding the cake to create the effect of a bottom collar. If unsure of the technique used, see page 50. When icing is dry, pipe a picot edge to runout using a no. 1 tube (tip) and dark pink royal icing.

● Pipe a small shell border around base of cake where it meets runout, using a no. 3 tube (tip) and pink royal icing. Fix 6 small clusters of roses to board runout at base of cake as illustrated opposite. Trace inscription on page 63; scribe on cake top. Using a no.1 tube (tip) and dark pink icing, pipe inscription. Prepare to fix top collar in place by piping a line just inside top edge of cake, using pale pink icing and a no. 2 tube. Carefully attach top collar. Fill any gaps between cake surface and runout with icing, using a no. 1 tube; smooth off with a damp paintbrush or small plastic squeegee.

● Neaten underside of runout with a row of small piped shells at angle where runouts meets cake side. Using a no. 1 tube (tip) and dark pink icing, pipe a picot line on cake top just inside collar edge. Arrange some sugar or silk roses around base of heart ornament. Using a little icing, fix ornament to cake top. With a no.1 tube and pale pink icing, pipe a tiny shell border around top edge of board. Trim board edge.

EXPERT ADVICE
≈
To achieve a marbled effect in runout, have ready a bag of run-icing fitted with a no. 1 tube (tip) and filled with icing of a deeper shade than that used for the runout. You will also require a fine paintbrush with the tip squeezed to a chisel head, or a fine-pointed scriber. As soon as runout flooding is complete, and before it has started to dry, pipe a continuous line 5mm (¼ in) inside outer edge. Stroke paintbrush or other implement through coloured line at regular intervals, as when feathering glacé icing, cleaning implement after each stroke. Leave to dry in usual way.

SILENT NIGHT

*D*eep blue is not an easy colour to work with in food but its use in creating a natural-looking night sky does not detract from the appetising appearance of this cake.

20cm (8 in) square cake
apricot glaze
875g (1¾ lb) marzipan (almond paste)
200g (7 oz) blue royal icing
500g (1 lb) white royal icing
selection of food colourings
albumen solution for run-icing
caster (superfine) sugar
snowflake dusting powder
(petal dust/blossom tint)
EQUIPMENT
25cm (10 in) cake board
runout equipment, see page 6
no. 1, 2, 3 and 8 or 9 piping tubes (tips)
about 1m (1 yd 3 in) ribbon for cake sides
about 1.25m (1¼ yd) ribbon or paper band for board edge

● Brush cake with apricot glaze and cover with marzipan (almond paste). Coat top of cake with deep blue royal icing, then coat sides and board with white royal icing, see Expert Advice.

● Using templates on page 64 and technique for outlined figures on pages 16-17, make runouts of village scene and fir bough. Flood lower part of fir bough first, using green run-icing, then flood upper part. When dry, pipe needle effect on green bough, using pale green royal icing and a no. 1 tube (tip). Add red berries, using a no. 1 tube. When top half of bough is dry, use white royal icing and a small shell tube to pipe on snow effect. Roughen texture with paintbrush. Sprinkle with caster (superfine) sugar and allow to dry.

● Flood houses and church in village scene in terracota run-icing, then flood rooftops in white.

When houses are dry, pipe on windows using yellow royal icing and a no. 1 tube. When rooftops are dry, brush them with snowflake dusting powder (petal dust/blossom tint).

● Pipe upright shell border around base of cake, using white royal icing and a no. 8 or 9 shell tube (tip). Overpipe with interlocking dropped loops, using a no. 2 tube.

● Fix village runout on cake top, using a little icing on the reverse. With a no. 1 tube (tip) and yellow royal icing, pipe stars at random in the night sky. Pipe a crescent moon.

● Carefully reverse fir bough runout on a block of foam. Pipe a line 5mm (¼ in) inside edge, using a no. 3 tube (tip). Allow line to dry, then overpipe using the same tube. Carefully position runout on cake top so that it stands a little proud of the surface.

● Pipe a top border of simple shells with a no. 8 or 9 shell tube (tip) and white royal icing. Complete the cake with a red ribbon around the sides. Trim the board edge with ribbon or a paper band.

EXPERT ADVICE

≈

To keep cake edges clean when coating in two different colours, complete all coats in the deeper colour first, then coat in the lighter shade, taking care not to get too much icing on the dark section.

TEMPLATES

Plaque Shapes

*Make 3 for
Twin Heart Engagement Cake*

Heart ornament

Plaque for heart ornament

Plaque for numerals

Numerals for Coming Of Age Cake

Easter Cake

St Patrick's Day Cake

st. patrick's day

Embroidery pattern for Christening Cake

58

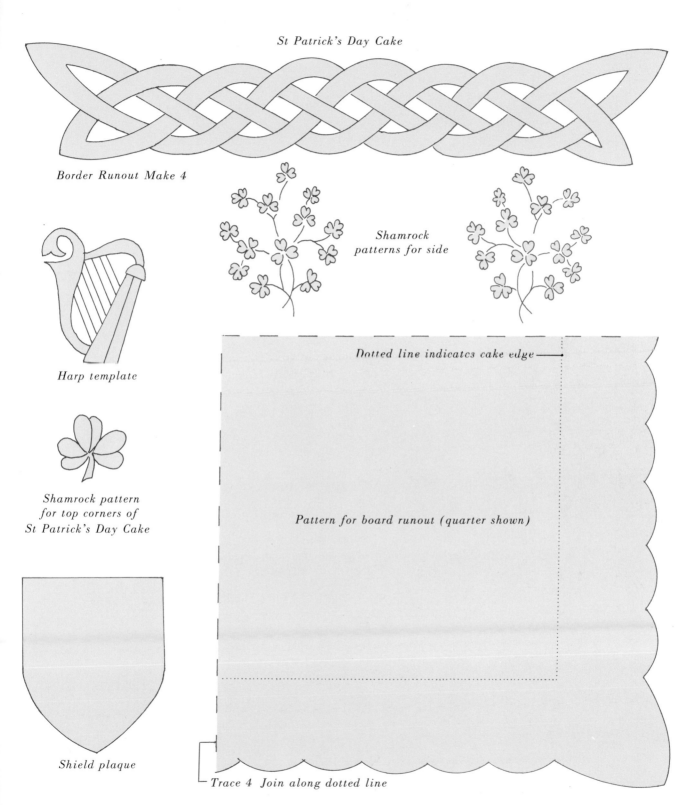

St Patrick's Day Cake

Border Runout Make 4

Harp template

Shamrock patterns for side

Shamrock pattern
for top corners of
St Patrick's Day Cake

Shield plaque

Dotted line indicates cake edge

Pattern for board runout (quarter shown)

Trace 4 Join along dotted line

Bon Voyage Cake

Side and top runouts   Make 8

Side runout Make 8

Template of tree outlines

Balloon and basket runouts   Make 2 of each

Inscription

Bon Voyage...

Dad's Birthday Cake

*Corner pieces
Make 2 of each*

Happy
Birthday
DAD

Happy Christmas!

Inscription for Christmas Cake

Anniversary Cake

Flower barrow
Broken line shows position of
piped line for fixing to cake

Plant pot

Barrow handle

Barrow wheel

Inscription

Happy Anniversary

Broken line indicates cake edge

Section for top border
Make 6

Overlay
Make 6

Patterns for side linework

Section for bottom border
Make 6

Valentine's Day Cake

Line shows cake edge

Inscription

With love Valentine

Pattern for side design

Full collar (half shown)
Trace twice and join at broken line

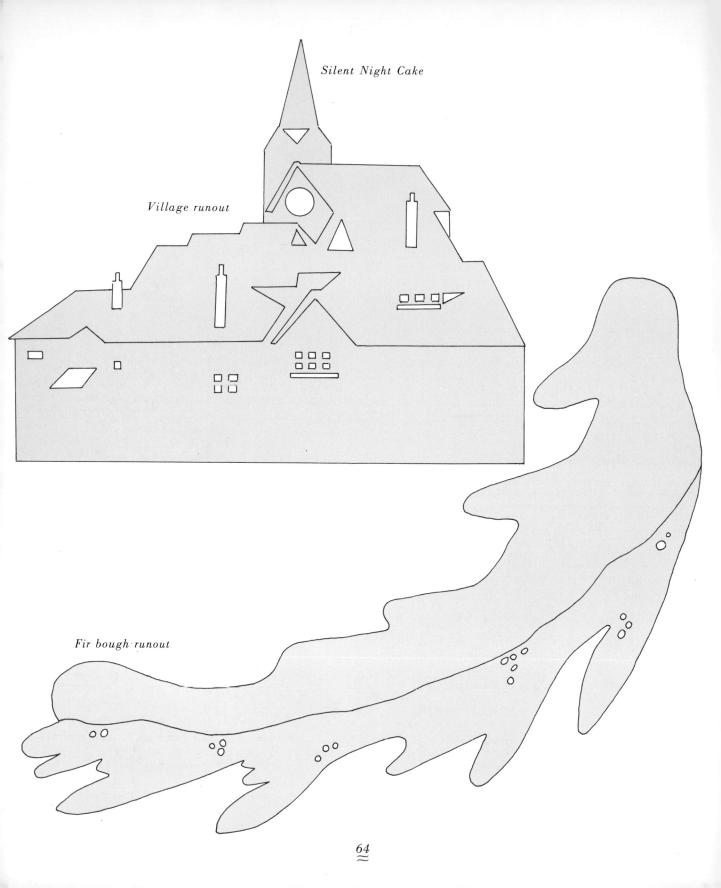

Silent Night Cake

Village runout

Fir bough runout

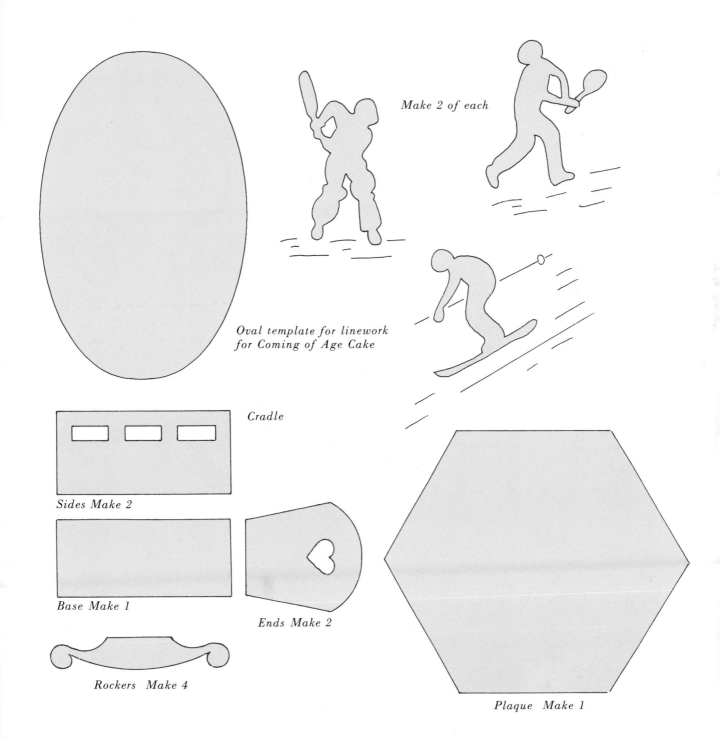

Coming of Age Cake

Make 2 of each

Oval template for linework
for Coming of Age Cake

Cradle

Sides Make 2

Base Make 1

Ends Make 2

Rockers Make 4

Plaque Make 1

ABCDE

FGHIJK

LMNOP

QRSTU

Continued on page 67

V W W X Y Z

Alphabet for Judo Cake

A B C D E F
G H I J K L M
N O P Q R S T
U V W X Y Z

ABCDEFGHIJKLM

NOPQRSTUVWXYZ

abcdefghijklmn

opqrstuvwxyz

1234567890

ABCDEFGH

IJKLMNOPQ

RSTUVWXYZ

1234567890

*M*istakes do happen - even to the most experienced sugarcraft artists! Here is a short list of some common problems, with a few face-saving solutions.

RUNOUT LOOKS LUMPY

Check consistency of sugar - the runout is probably starting to dry before flooding has been completed.

RUNOUT WILL NOT DRY

If a runout has not dried in 24 hours, throw it away. Even if you succeed in drying it after that time it will not have a good gloss and will look dull and heavy. The fault may lie with your recipe: weak albumen, old icing, icing insufficiently beaten. Unsuitable drying conditions (not warm enough) may be a contributory factor, or perhaps there were traces of grease on the equipment used. See also glycerol (glycerine), in Glossary opposite.

CRACKED SURFACE

The wax paper has probably been moved after drying has commenced and before it has been completed.

RUNOUT CRUMBLES WHEN REMOVED FROM PAPER

The albumen used may have been weak. If the fault occurs on a coloured runout, it may be because too much colour has been used.

DULL, HEAVY-LOOKING APPEARANCE

The icing may not have been beaten enough or it may have been too old. Alternatively, too much colour may have been used or drying was too slow.

COLOUR MIGRATION/PATCHY COLOUR

Colour was not properly mixed into icing; icing coloured after thinning instead of before; runout exposed to sunlight.

RUNOUT NOT FLAT

The drawing or wax paper may not have been perfectly smooth. Alternatively, the drying surface may have buckled under excessive heat.

RUNOUT STUCK TO PAPER

Too much heat has been applied, causing wax surface on paper to melt. Albumen strength incorrect.

REPAIRS

❖

Breakages do occur, so it is a good idea to make spares.

If runout figures break, it is usually at a join such as where the head meets the neck, or where a tail meets a body. To repair the break, position the main part of the figure, then pipe a dot or two of icing where the broken-off section is to go. Carefully butt it up against the larger piece. You will probably be unable to see the join.

If the break occurs after the runout has been positioned on the cake, try piping a little icing underneath the crack and brushing it out with a damp paintbrush.

Microdots broken off can be replaced, with care, but sections broken off completely are almost impossible to repair - find a spare, make another piece, or hope for inspiration!

AIRBRUSH A precision artist's instrument, consisting of a brush with liquid colour reservoir attached to a compressed air supply (canister or compressor). A finger trigger regulates the air flow from the compressor through the hose and colour reservoir to a tiny nozzle in the brush. Used by proficient sugarcraft artists for overall colour, creating designs or pictures, or adding shading on dry iced surfaces.

ALBUMEN POWDER Dried pasteurised egg white in powder form. Reconstituted in water, it can be used to make royal icing for runouts, see page 8. A valuable ingredient in runout work as a higher proportion of powder may be used than usual to create Run-icing, see right, with extra strength.

APRICOT GLAZE A smooth, clear coating made from boiled, sieved apricot jam. Frequently brushed over fruit cakes before covering with marzipan (almond paste). Other flavours may be used for glazes, but apricot is regarded as having a particular affinity for marzipan.

COLLAR A delicate runout usually extending beyond the edge of a cake. Can have open sections. See also pages 50-51.

CORNELLI WORK A method of piping in controlled wavy lines. Sometimes referred to as scribbling. Royal icing is used and the aim is to produce long continuous lines which look like random squiggles but which loop back on themselves to create a delicate effect.

CRIMPERS Implements, usually metal, used to mark designs in soft sugarpaste or marzipan (almond paste).

DUSTING POWDER (PETAL DUST/BLOSSOM TINT) Fine powders in dark or pale colours. Used on runout plaques and lettering to create shading, backgrounds or variations in colour.

EMBOSSING TOOLS Implements with relief designs used to stamp patterns in soft sugarpaste; perfectly clean buttons or badges may be used.

FLOODING As the name suggests, this means to cover an area with icing. Special icing (see Run-icing, right) is used in a piping bag which may or may not be fitted with a tube (tip). See also page 8.

GARRETT FRILLS Sugarpaste frills applied to side of cake. Special cutters are available from cake decorating shops.

GLYCEROL (GLYCERINE) Colourless, odourless sweet liquid used in paste colours and piping gel to prevent drying out. Such colours should be used with caution for runout work, where efficient drying out is essential.

MONOGRAMS Letters linked together in an artistic fashion. Often used on engagement or wedding cakes.

OVERPIPING A technique where successive lines, each thinner than the last, are built up on top of -or very close to - each other to create a sculptured effect.

PIPING GEL Clear jelly-like substance which liquifies on being warmed. Used on its own to pipe designs on royal icing or sugarpaste, it can also be coloured. Also added to royal icing to slow down the drying process and make it more elastic.

RUN-ICING Royal icing which has been strengthened by additional albumen and thinned so that it flows readily to cover a given area. See also page 8.

WAFER FLOWERS Wafer-thin edible cake decorations, usually roses.

INDEX

FOR FURTHER INFORMATION

Merehurst is the leading publisher of cake decorating books and has an excellent range of titles to suit all levels. Please send for our free catalogue, stating the title of this book:-

United Kingdom
*Marketing Department
Merehurst Ltd.
Ferry House
51-57 Lacy Road
London SW15 1PR
Tel: 081 780 1177
Fax: 081 780 1714*

U.S.A.
*Sterling Publishing Co.
Inc.
387 Park Avenue South
New York
NY 10016-8810, USA
Tel: (1) 212 532 7160
Fax: (1) 212 213 2495*

Australia
*J.B. Fairfax Press Pty.
Ltd.
80 McLachlan Avenue
Rushcutters Bay
NSW 2011
Tel: (61) 2 361 6366
Fax: (61) 2 360 6262*

Other Territories
*For further information
contact:
International Sales
Department at United
Kingdom address.*